After the wedding, the bride's father remarked that it was 'just as unreal as a fairy tale.' And so it was. A German commoner had just married the King of Sweden.

The Swedish people loved their new Queen. But throughout a long courtship, there had been doubts as to whether the marriage would happen. Love, however, triumphed.

DIFFERENT BACKGROUNDS

Hulton Picture Company

♛ *Prince Carl Gustaf was the youngest of five children. At the age of six months he was photographed with his sister, Christina above*

STOCKHOLM REJOICED WHEN A PRINCE WAS BORN, THOUGH IT SEEMED MANY YEARS BEFORE HE WOULD RULE. MEANWHILE, A YOUNG GERMAN GIRL, WHO WOULD GROW UP IN BRAZIL, WAS DESTINED TO VISIT SWEDEN

Pressens Bild

♛ *Four generations of royalty gather for an official portrait above. King Gustaf V holds his great-grandson while Crown Prince Gustaf Adolph (in glasses) and the young Prince's father look on proudly*

'Oh, a Prince at last!'

PRINCESS CHRISTINA

A FIFTH CHILD WAS BORN TO PRINCE Gustaf Adolf and Princess Sibylla on 30 April 1946. When the 42-gun salute thundered out over Stockholm a jubilant cheer rang out. Sweden had a Prince who would one day be King. The little Prince was especially welcome, as only males could succeed to the throne of Sweden.

The woman who had just given birth could scarcely believe it was true – she had tried so hard for a son. Her three-year-old daughter, Princess Christina, cried out in delight: 'Oh, a Prince at last!'

Gustaf Adolf and Sibylla had been married for 14 years when the Prince was born. They already had four daughters. The first, Margaretha, was born in 1934, Birgitta in 1937, Désirée a year later and then Christina in 1943.

The Prince was named Carl Gustaf Folke Hubertus. He was carried forward at the christening ceremony by his great-grandfather, the reigning King, Gustaf V. Carl Gustaf was third in line to the throne, after his grandfather, Crown Prince Gustaf Adolf, and his father, Prince Gustaf Adolf. It seemed likely that he would be an elderly man by the time he became King.

The Prince's parents

The young Prince's father, Gustaf Adolf, had met his future wife at a London wedding. Princess Sibylla of Saxe-Coburg-Gotha was a bridesmaid when Lady May Cambridge, a niece of Queen Mary, married Captain Henry Abel Smith. Barely a year later, in 1932, Prince Gustaf Adolf and Sibylla were married in Coburg, the Princess's home town. Adolf Hilter was an honorary citizen of the town and the Nazi insignia to be seen at the wedding added a sour note to the festivities.

When war broke out in 1939, the Princess's German background made her unpopular, and many people accused her of harbouring Nazi sympathies. She took this criticism very much to heart, and, as a result, it coloured her relationship with the people of Sweden from then on.

Prince Gustaf Adolf, on the other hand, had grown up in a family which had a pronounced English character. His mother, Princess Margareta, was the daughter of the Duke of Connaught, and the family spent part of each summer in England. All the children were encouraged to devote themselves to sports and athletics. The young Gustaf Adolf became a distinguished competition horseman and swordsman, winning several championships.

Sibylla shared Gustaf Adolf's interest in hunting and other outdoor pursuits, and they bought a mountain chalet in Storlien, where they celebrated Easter with their children each

Hulton Picture Company

Popperfoto

Pressens Bild

year. The present Royal couple maintain this tradition and continue to take an annual skiing holiday in the mountains.

Settling into Haga Palace

Gustaf Adolf and Sibylla made their home at Haga Palace, just outside Stockholm, and it proved to be an ideal place for a family with children. The Palace itself is quite small, with bright cheerful rooms, but it stands in very extensive grounds. The children could play there without being disturbed and the Royal couple led a fairly quiet family life.

They were not particularly popular with the Swedish people. Gustaf Adolf was shy and reserved by nature, while Princess Sibylla found it difficult to relate to her new countrymen because of her inability to learn Swedish.

However, public sympathy for the family at Haga grew as the number of children in it increased. After all, who can resist a quartet of charming, fair-haired Princesses?

The birth of the Prince was a happy event, not only for the Royal Family but for the whole of Sweden, and he quickly became the centre of attention. His great-grandfather saw to it that a good nurse was engaged. His parents took it in turns to feed him and his sisters helped to rock his cot.

Just in time for Christmas, 'The Duke', as he was affectionately known, cut his first teeth. The following January, on his sister Birgitta's birthday, he said 'pappa' for the first time.

Tragedy strikes

The family's happiness was short-lived. Just a few days later, on 26 January 1947, Gustaf Adolf was killed. He was on his way home from a hunting party in Holland, where he had been a guest of Prince Bernhard of the Netherlands, when his plane crashed at Kastrup Airport, killing everyone on board.

Grief at the loss of the Prince hung heavy over Haga. The four Princesses missed their father terribly, but the baby Prince was just nine months old and was too young to be aware of his loss.

King Gustaf V was aged 89 and Crown Prince Gustaf Adolf was 65 when the accident occurred. It was clear now that Carl Gustaf would become a young King, and this fact influenced his entire childhood.

Father-figures

The task of rearing her son to kingship was a heavy burden for Princess Sibylla to bear alone. She realized that he would lack a father-figure, so during his entire childhood she tried to compensate for this by sharing his interests as fully as possible. His grandfather, the Crown Prince, played an important part in his development, but he was already an elderly man. It was Prince Bertil, the Prince's uncle, who assumed

♛ *Prince Carl Gustaf was the cossetted darling of his family. After the death of his father, he proved a great consolation to his mother above far left, while his sunny disposition and good looks endeared him to the whole nation above left. Carl Gustaf's four elder sisters above left to right Margaretha, Birgitta, Desirée and Christina, all doted on him*

♛ *King Gustaf V died when Carl Gustaf was just four years old. The new Crown Prince and his family moved into the Royal Palace in Stockholm. There, he continued his early interest in all things mechanical. The bustle of the city, its traffic and building works fascinated him, and he loved to play with toy trucks and bulldozers below*

Popperfoto

Popperfoto

Hulton Picture Company

the role of stand-in father.

It was Sibylla's wish that Carl Gustaf should enjoy a relatively normal childhood. She did all she could to prevent him from being cosseted. For this reason, she was often a rather strict mother, even though, in her heart of hearts, she was very fond of her son. Despite her efforts, the young Prince became the pet of the whole family and his sisters were completely at his beck and call.

Carl Gustaf's golden locks and big blue eyes gave him a doll-like charm. He quickly became the darling of the Swedish people. Initially, he was rather shy and was embarrassed by the public attention he received. At Haga Palace, however, the Prince could be kept out of the public eye for much of the time.

A lively child

At home, he was an extremely lively child. His nanny, Ingrid Björnberg, had a hard time keeping her eye on him. She later admitted that she was terrified at the thought that something might happen to him. He was, after all, a future

'I'm not going to be King, I'm going to be a workman'

YOUNG CARL GUSTAF

heir to the throne and, apart from his uncle Bertil, was the only one who could continue the monarchy.

His sister Christina was his dearest playmate. It soon became apparent that the Prince was practical by nature. As long as he had a plank of wood, a hammer and a few nails he could amuse himself for hours. He loved digging in the garden and was fascinated by mechanical toys of any kind. He was serenely happy when the Palace chauffeur allowed him to pretend to drive the car.

On one occasion, when his big sister Christina told him that he would one day be King, he gave her a hefty clout.

'I'm not going to be King, I'm going to be a workman,' he explained angrily.

Becoming Crown Prince

When Carl Gustaf was four the whole family moved into the Royal Palace in Stockholm, while Haga was being restored. That autumn, King Gustaf V died at the age of 92. Carl Gustaf's grandfather, now aged 68, acceded to the throne, and Carl Gustaf became Crown Prince and next in line. King Gustaf VI Adolf received the homage of his people from the palace balcony, with the Crown Prince held in his arms.

♛ *From the age of five, the Crown Prince and his mother accompanied King Gustaf VI on state occasions, such as the celebrations of Sweden's National Day on June 6* top. *At home in the Palace, his mother attempted to harness his practical impulses by teaching him crafts* above, *but it was soon time for him to begin his formal schooling as a day boy at Anna Broms's private school in Stockholm* left

Popperfoto

For practical reasons, it was decided that Sibylla and the five children should continue to live at the Royal Palace. Naturally, the children missed the grounds and gardens of Haga, where they used to have sleigh rides in winter. There, too, they had been free to wander about at will, without having to bother about avoiding traffic or crowds.

But a new world was revealed to the Prince. He could sit at a window for hours watching the cars and trams go by. He loved machines. When he was taken for walks by his nanny he was most fascinated by building sites, with their excavators and cranes. And his happiness was complete if he was allowed to buy a hot dog at a street stall.

Starting school

A nursery school with six other children was started at the Palace, so that the Prince could get used to being with other children. When the time came for him to attend a normal school it was decided that he should start at Ann Broms's Private School in central Stockholm. This school was also attended by the children of many of the Royal couple's friends.

It was, of course, a great adventure for Carl

♚ **At the Broms school, Carl Gustaf proved a keen and able athlete** above. When he was 13, he left home for the first time, to board at Sigtuna College, a grammar school not far from Stockholm right

Hulton Picture Company

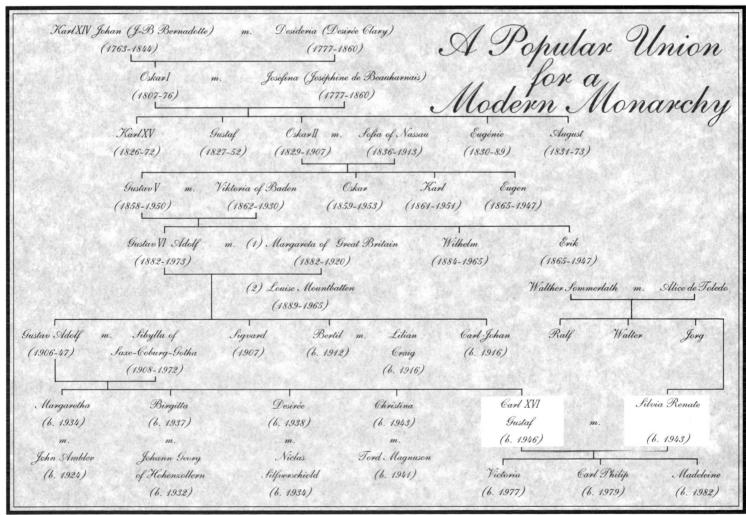

A Popular Union for a Modern Monarchy

Karl XIV Johan (J-B Bernadotte) (1763-1844)	m.	Desideria (Desirée Clary) (1777-1860)			
Oskar I (1807-76)	m.	Josefina (Joséphine de Beauharnais) (1777-1860)			
Karl XV (1826-72)	Gustaf (1827-52)	Oskar II m. (1829-1907)	Sofia of Nassau (1836-1913)	Eugénie (1830-89)	August (1831-73)
Gustav V m. (1858-1950)	Viktoria of Baden (1862-1930)	Oskar (1859-1953)	Karl (1861-1951)	Eugen (1865-1947)	
Gustav VI Adolf m. (1) (1882-1973)	Margareta of Great Britain (1882-1920)		Wilhelm (1884-1965)	Erik (1865-1947)	
	(2) Louise Mountbatten (1889-1965)			Walther Sommerlath m. Alice de Toledo	
Gustav Adolf m. Sibylla of (1906-47) Saxe-Coburg-Gotha (1908-1972)	Sigvard (1907)	Bertil m. Lilian (b. 1912) Craig (b. 1916)	Carl Johan (b. 1916)	Ralf Walter Jörg	
Margaretha (b. 1934) m. John Ambler (b. 1924)	Birgitta (b. 1937) m. Johann Georg of Hohenzollern (b. 1932)	Desirée (b. 1938) m. Niclas Silfverschiold (b. 1934)	Christina (b. 1943) m. Tord Magnuson (b. 1941)	Carl XVI Gustaf (b. 1946) m.	Silvia Renate (b. 1943)
				Victoria (b. 1977) Carl Philip (b. 1979)	Madeleine (b. 1982)

Gustaf to leave his secluded world and meet boys of his own age. Though he was a live wire at home, he was fairly shy among his new schoolfriends. He certainly envied the freedom the other children had. After school, they could do as they wished, but the Prince was always fetched by a private chauffeur and kept under surveillance.

People naturally felt sorry for him, but there was little they could do. They never dared take any risks for fear that something would happen to the Prince.

On the death of his great-grandfather, the young Prince had inherited Solliden, a beautiful, palatial villa on the island of Öland. It had been built in the Italian style by his great-grandmother, Queen Viktoria of Sweden. Solliden looks out across the Baltic. The landscaped grounds and well-kept gardens are a celebrated beauty spot and are open to the public a few hours each day. Solliden became a veritable summer paradise for Sibylla and her children. This was a place where they could all relax and enjoy a measure of freedom.

At Solliden, the Prince learned to ride, swim and sail. Princess Sibylla loved the island's unique scenery and taught her children to appreciate the unusual plants and birds of Öland. These early summers gave the Prince a lasting interest in the countryside and the environment, which he, in turn, has passed on to his children.

Choosing a new school

The question of the Prince's education and upbringing was not purely a private one. An advisory council was set up, comprising his grandfather, Gustaf VI Adolf, Prince Bertil, and the 'Three Wise Men', Lieutenant-General Malcolm Murray, Baron Ramel and the Chief Comptroller, Carl Eric Ekstrand. They decided that the Prince should attend a public school so that he could enjoy normal contact with other children of his age.

His father and uncle had been educated at Lundsberg, in the province of Värmland, a public school which admitted boys only. But Sibylla wanted to have her son nearer to Stockholm, so it was agreed to send him to Sigtuna Grammar School. This school had mixed classes of boys and girls and was attended by local children from the charming little town of Sigtuna on Lake Mälaren.

The Prince enjoyed complete freedom at Sigtuna, and was able to cycle in the peaceful streets, go to the cinema and visit his schoolfriends in their homes. Instructions were issued that the Prince should be treated in precisely the same way as all other pupils. He was not to be granted any special privileges.

Carl Gustaf enjoyed himself at Sigtuna. He

👑 *Prince Carl Gustaf spent the summer before he began at Sigtuna camping with his Boy Scout troop on an offshore island near Stockholm* above and inset. *He had* *earlier learned from his mother to appreciate the outdoor life. In his early teens he was trained as a yachtsman at a sailing school at Lokholmen* below

6

Popperfoto

was by no means a swot, but he was good at games and athletics. His friends called him 'Tjabo' and he felt at ease with them. He was very popular and the gang protected him loyally from undue public attention and from inquisitive newspaper reporters.

Press speculation

As time passed the attentions of the Press grew increasingly embarrassing. The papers started speculating as to which European Princess would become the Prince's wife. The girls in his circle of acquaintances were pointed out as objects of his tender affections. It could not have been easy for a shy teenager to accept that each and every girl he danced with was presented in the following day's papers as 'the Crown Prince's girlfriend'. The Prince felt particularly sorry for the girls.

The marriage rumours were to circulate for over ten years. In time the Prince learned to be on his guard. He became adept at avoiding Press photographers and the girls he knew enjoyed helping him. His friends were unswervingly loyal, and anyone who gossiped was immediately banned from the gang.

A radiantly happy Carl Gustaf passed his university entrance exams in 1966. He was tossed aloft by his friends and was congratulated by the King and by his mother and sisters. A few hundred Press photographers also turned up to record his matriculation. His marks were admittedly not all that good, but they were good enough, and the Prince had never pretended to be academically inclined.

Hulton Picture Company

♛ *When he was 16, the Crown Prince above centre was one of 14 young people confirmed in the Lutheran Church of Sweden at a ceremony in Borgholm, Öland. Three years later, there was a less formal ceremony when he passed his university entrance examinations. His fellow-students chaired him to the Palace below for an 'open house' party hosted by his mother and the King right*

Popperfoto

Pressens Bild

A FUTURE QUEEN IS BORN

Silvia Sommerlath was born in Heidelberg, Germany, on 23 December 1943. This was at the height of World War 2, when Allied bombs were raining down on the country. As there was no transport to be had, Walther Sommerlath took his wife by the arm and walked her to Dr. Erna Glaesmer's private clinic early in the morning. The delivery was uneventful and the family celebrated Christmas in an atmosphere of happiness and thankfulness. The Sommerlaths had three sons already, so the little girl was particularly welcome.

♛ *Silvia Sommerlath was born into a ready-made family of three brothers above left to right Jorg, Ralf and Walther. When she was three, her father, Walther below, took his family back to Brazil, where Silvia grew up speaking Portuguese as her first language*

Svenskt Pressfoto

She was christened Silvia Renate. Her first home was a five-room flat at 28 Dantestrasse, which the Sommerlaths shared with another family until the end of the war.

It was simple bad luck that the family happened to be in Germany during the war. In the 1920s Walther had left his homeland to seek his fortune as a young engineer in Brazil. In Rio de Janeiro he met his future wife, Alice de Toledo, a beautiful girl of Spanish descent whose family owned extensive estates in Brazil. They were married three years later and settled in São Paulo, where their sons Ralf and Walther were born. Walther Sommerlath represented a German steel mill and was building a good career in his new homeland.

His wife Alice, though, was frail and, according to her doctors, the warm climate of her native land was not good for her. In 1937 the family left South America and made its way back to Berlin, where Walther Sommerlath founded a company for manufacturing electrical components.

Bombed out

When war broke out, Alice and the children moved from the capital to Heidelberg. Shortly afterwards, their house in Berlin was bombed and the factory was subsequently destroyed. Walther Sommerlath joined his family in Heidelberg and spent the war years there.

Despite the hard times, the Sommerlath family was relatively fortunate. Heidelberg escaped the bombing and Walther was not called up. A son, Jörg, was born in 1941 and Silvia arrived two years later. She brightened up the dark times and the boys tried to outdo each other in spoiling her.

When the war ended, the family was destitute but intact. Silvia remembers nothing of the war years. She was aged three when the family returned to Brazil. Her father became sales director for the Swedish Uddeholm concern, and the family bought a beautiful pink house in São Paulo.

A happy family

This was where Silvia grew up. The dark years were quickly forgotten. The family soon prospered again and Silvia had everything she could wish for. Her brothers were her playmates and guardians. It was from them she learned how to be bold and not to give in without a struggle, despite the fact that she was the youngest child and the only girl.

They were a close and happy family. Alice Sommerlath had numerous lively relatives who visited them frequently and made a great fuss of little Silvia.

Alice and Walther were keen to ensure that their children should be independent and learn

THE FIRST BERNADOTTE

The beginnings of Sweden's democratic monarchy go back to 1810, when the Swedish crown was offered to one of Napoleon's most able marshals, Jean-Baptiste Bernadotte *right*. He was chosen because the Swedish King Carl XIII had no heirs. After obtaining Napoleon's permission, Bernadotte accepted the proposition in 1810. He quickly took up the cause of Sweden and converted to Lutherism on his way north to Sweden. He took over state affairs when the King had a stroke, and ascended the throne in 1818 as Carl XIV Johan. He had earlier married Désirée Clary, whose sister married Napoleon's brother, and who was herself the Emperor's first love. Bernadotte and his wife founded the new dynasty of which King Carl XVI Gustaf is a direct descendant

Bridgeman Art Library

🜲 *Silvia grew into a likeable teenager. A much-loved companion was a pet monkey* below *that her father bought for her while he was on a sales trip*

her classmates tittered at her quaint accent. Silvia felt like a lonely outsider and it was years before she felt at home in Germany.

The Sommerlaths lived in a Swedish-built house outside Düsseldorf and Silvia started here at Luisenschule. Having spent ten years of her life in Brazil, her experiences and background differed completely from those of her friends. Her father or brothers would take her to parties and call for her at a set time. Silvia found this quite normal, but her friends thought her parents were unusually strict.

Visiting Sweden

Working as he did for a Swedish company, Walther Sommerlath frequently travelled to Sweden. One summer he took Silvia and her mother on a trip to the Swedish province of Värmland. Silvia was fascinated by the country.

For many years Silvia's favourite book was to be *Désirée*, the story of Napoleon's one-time fiancée, Désirée Clary. Désirée's family prevented her from marrying Napoleon and she subsequently married one of his marshals, Jean-Baptiste Bernadotte. Marshal Bernadotte was chosen by Napoleon as successor to the throne of Sweden and, when he became King, Désirée became Queen of Sweden. Crown Prince Carl Gustaf was one of her descendants.

how to shoulder responsibility. They had a strict but loving upbringing, and Silvia has often mentioned the atmosphere of friendliness and affection that pervaded her home.

Silvia attended a German private school when she lived in Brazil. Her chief interests were music and drawing. She was a very charming and spontaneous girl and was liked by everyone. Walther was extremely fond of his daughter and affectionately called her 'Kätzchen' (Kitten). He always brought presents with him when he returned from his sales trips, and the one she appreciated most was a cheeky little monkey with which she played in the villa's tropical garden.

Back to Germany

The Swedish firm offered Walther Sommerlath a job in Düsseldorf, which he accepted. Once again, the reason for returning to Germany was his wife's failing health. It was with a heavy heart that Silvia said goodbye to her relatives and schoolfriends. Of course, she looked forward eagerly to the tour of Europe her father had promised her, but the thought of going to a new school and speaking another language worried her. She was 13 when the family arrived back in Germany.

Silvia spent her first year at a private school in Heidelberg, to improve her German. At school she was considered rather exotic and

Svenskt Pressfoto

Pressens Bild

Popperfoto

♛ *Carl Gustaf was born into a ready-made family of four girls above, all of whom were anxious to spoil him*

Popperfoto

♛ *From the moment he took his first steps, the Prince loved to play with carts and trucks above*

♛ *At the age of two, he rode his trike round the Haga Palace left*

♛ *Aged three, the Prince graduated to four wheels below*

Popperfoto

Popperfoto

♛ *The three-year-old Prince with his great-grandfather, Gustaf V*

Silvia

👑 **Baby Silvia in the arms of her South American-born mother, Alice** above

👑 *Silvia as a toddler in the garden at Heidelberg* above

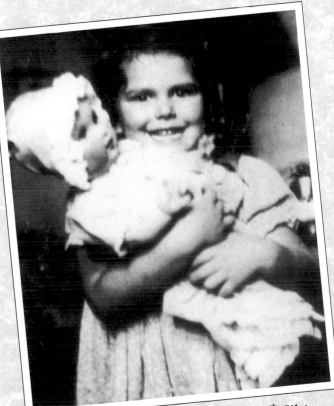

👑 *Silvia and a favourite doll*

👑 *Growing up in Brazil with her youngest brother Jörg* above

STATE REGALIA

TREASURES FROM THE 16TH CENTURY

The State regalia of Sweden is relatively young by European standards and dates from the revival of the Swedish monarchy under the Vasa dynasty in the 16th century. The Vasa kings and their successors assembled a magnificent, complete set of Coronation emblems. These now belong to the state

Treasury, Royal Palace, Stockholm

This magnificent crown of silver and diamonds *above* was made for Queen Lovisa Ulrika, wife of King Adolf Frederik whose Coronation took place in 1751. The Queen later attempted to pawn the diamonds to finance a political intrigue but was forced to recover them and reinstate them

Pressens Bild

At his enthronement in 1973, King Carl Gustaf *above* sits on the silver throne especially made for the Coronation of the legendary Queen Christina of Sweden in 1650. The throne, which was a gift to the Queen, has been used by all her successors

The crown, orb, sceptre and key of State *right* were made for the Coronation of Eric XIV in 1560. The second of the Vasa kings, Eric hoped to bolster the prestige of the new dynasty by making his Coronation and the regalia as impressive as possible

♔ Queen Silvia *below* wears an unusual set of necklace, tiara and earrings inset with antique cameos. These pieces once belonged to Queen Josefina of Sweden, the granddaughter of Napoleon's Empress, Josephine de Beauharnais, to whom the cameos may have originally belonged

♔ Another item of jewellery which has been passed down through successive generations of the Swedish Royal Family is the parure of tourmalines and diamonds worn by the Queen *left*. Like the cameo set, this belonged to the Beauharnais family

♔ This Royal cradle *below* was first used by King Carl XI, who ruled 1672-1697. Swedish Royal babies were traditionally presented to the Court in this cradle. Photographs of Prince Carl Philip's christening in 1979 show him in this intricately carved object

Pressens Bild

Treasury, Royal Palace, Stockholm

Reginald Davis

Popperfoto

IT JUST CLICKED

AS HE TRAINED TO BE KING, CARL GUSTAF WORKED HARD AND PLAYED HARD. SILVIA WORKED AT THE OLYMPICS. IT WAS LOVE AT FIRST SIGHT WHEN SHE MET THE PRINCE BUT THE ROMANCE WAS BESET BY PROBLEMS

Popperfoto

👑 *When they met at the 1972 Olympics in Germany, the 25-year-old Crown Prince above was one of the most eligible bachelors in Europe. From the moment he laid eyes on her, he lost his heart to the dark-haired, vivacious Silvia above right, who was three years his senior*

👑 *Carl Gustaf's spell of military service was spent mainly in the Navy, at his own choice. There he was able to pursue his love of sailing; in 1966, aboard the* Falken, *he took part in the Tall Ships race from Falmouth below*

FOR CARL GUSTAF'S SCHOOLFELLOWS matriculation was a door to adult life and freedom. Freedom, however, was not on the Crown Prince's agenda. His future had been carefully mapped out for him and was planned in the minutest detail. He had to continue his training for kingship.

His first duty was to undergo his military service. At the Prince's express wish the bulk of his training was to be done in the Navy. He was enrolled as Midshipman 001 at the Royal Naval College in the summer of 1966. In the autumn, he left Sweden on a world cruise on board the mine-hunter *H.M.S. Alvsnabben*.

His life on board was the same as that of any other midshipman, and he had to wash the decks and do his share of rust scraping. But when the ship put into port, and his fellow sailors went ashore to enjoy themselves, the Prince was received by governors and ambassadors. Under the watchful eye of security guards, he had to make official calls and hold Press conferences.

By the end of the voyage the Crown Prince had learned seamanship and had received good grounding in representing Sweden. He had also matured and acquired greater confidence.

A tough schedule

Following his spell in the Navy, he received training in the Army and the Air Force. He learned to handle small arms and to drive armoured cars and, on rigorous route marches through the mountains, he mastered the art of erecting a bivouac in rough weather. The Air Force taught him to fly a military plane and put him through his first parachute jump.

After two years' training the Prince passed his naval officer examination. He was Sweden's only fourfold Ensign, holding that rank in the Svea Lifeguards, the Jämtland Rifles, the Navy and the Air Force.

A year of studies now lay ahead of him at the University of Uppsala. Following a specially devised curriculum, he read economics, political science, fiscal law, sociology and history. He shared a student flat in Uppsala with a few good friends. When he returned to Stockholm he was given his own apartment at the Palace.

In Sweden an heir-apparent does not come of age until he is 25, and the young Carl Gustaf wielded very little power. His education continued apace, in accordance with a very rigorous programme. The Prince continued his studies at the University of Stockholm. He also made study tours abroad and worked for short periods in various civil service departments and industrial concerns. The aim was to give him a general insight into the workings of the Swedish community.

Popperfoto

The King took an active interest in Carl Gustaf's upbringing and education. They grew very close and the Crown Prince later said how much he admired his grandfather. 'Grandfather taught me to see the positive things in life and people. He taught me how to listen to others, and that it is easier to resolve certain situations with a smile than with a lot of words.'

Despite his demanding schedule, Carl Gustaf found time for sport and for boisterous parties and outings with friends. When the Prince got his own apartment he was at last able to do whatever he wished in his leisure hours, and his mother was wise enough to give him a relatively free rein.

Having a good time

Carl Gustaf was extremely popular with the girls. He was handsome, good company and a fine dancer. In private he was neither shy nor stiff, and his colleagues described him as helpful, humorous and imaginative. The Prince liked an active life and detested idleness. He enjoyed fast boats and cars, and was also fond of

'Grandfather taught me to see the positive things in life and people'

CARL GUSTAF ON THE KING

having a good time at various discos.

The Crown Prince had several romances, but most of them remained unknown outside his own small circle of loyal and trusted friends. One or two relationships lasted a little longer than the others but there was nothing very serious in any of them.

Not surprisingly, his mother and sisters started looking round for a girl who might make a suitable wife. The problem was that only a girl of Royal descent could be considered a suitable match. The Prince's grandfather was inflexible on that point. Two of his own sons, Sigvard and Carl Johan, had been forced to renounce their Royal titles and privileges when they married commoners and Prince Bertil had to forgo marriage to a divorcee, Lilian Craig, for the same reason.

But the Crown Prince stubbornly answered every enquiry about marriage by saying that he intended to marry for love alone, whether or not the girl was a Princess.

Naturally, the Prince's lifestyle drew criticism. Many considered it unsuitable for a future King to behave like any ordinary young man,

♔ *Naval training was far from being all 'messing about in boats'. Drill was a major fact of life for the Crown Prince and his fellow cadets at Stockholm's Royal Naval Academy* above. *Following his stint in the Navy, Carl Gustaf went into the Army where he took part in military manoeuvres* right

♔ *At the passing-out parade for officer graduates from the Karlberg Military Academy in 1967 Carl Gustaf and his grandfather, the King, were photographed together in uniform for the first time* below

Popperfoto

Popperfoto

Popperfoto

15

but Sibylla defended him. 'Duties and responsibilities will come in due time, let him play and enjoy his youth,' she said.

Carl Gustaf's interest in sport led him to visit the Munich Olympic Games in the summer of 1972. The Crown Prince's journey was to change his life.

Silvia's studies

Silvia Sommerlath was very fond of children. In her final years at school in Düsseldorf she had plans to be a teacher. But she had an excellent ear for languages, and chose instead to study at the Sprachen und Dolmetscher Institut, in Munich, to become an interpreter. Four years later, in 1969, she received her Diploma in Spanish. She was also proficient in English, German, French and Portuguese.

Silvia had grown into a striking beauty with warm brown eyes, a dazzling smile and long dark hair. And there was no shortage of escorts. She went out with a young law student for a while but they ended the relationship. At that time Silvia was sharing a flat with two friends in

'Silvia is an exceptional person with a rare radiance'

WILLI DAUME, OLYMPIC VICE-PRESIDENT

the charming Schwabing district of Munich, where the majority of students lived. Following her examination, she worked at the Argentinian Consulate for two years. She was 28 and dreamed of meeting Mr. Right. She wanted to marry and raise a family.

An Olympic job

In preparation for the 1972 Munich Olympics, the Olympic Organization Committee advertised for hostesses. At the suggestion of a friend, Silvia applied. She was accepted, thanks to her excellent knowledge of languages, her charm and her efficiency. She so impressed the Committee that she was appointed Chief Hostess.

Her immediate superior, Dr. Emmy Schwabe, was full of praise for this beautiful girl who was so calm and efficient. Vice-President Willi Daume, of the International Olympic Committee, commented in glowing terms that 'She has a personality not often found in young people today. Silvia is an exceptional person with a rare radiance, great capacity and an impressive willpower beneath a soft exterior.'

Silvia thoroughly enjoyed her new job, de-

Popperfoto

Pressens Bild

Pressens Bild

Pressens Bild

♛ *The young Prince enjoyed the company of attractive women, and loved to dance. He was always in demand at parties, balls and other social occasions. Wherever he went, Press cameramen followed, and any girl photographed in his general vicinity* left *was presented in the Swedish newspapers as a potential future Queen. One person who benefited from such publicity was the actress Pia Degermark, who first came to the notice of the Swedish public when she danced with Carl Gustaf at a student ball* bottom left *and went on to star in Bo Wideberg's internationally-successful film* Elvira Madigan

spite the stress and the long hours involved. Silvia's talent for organization was soon noticed and she was given increasingly more responsibility. She was in charge of organizing the duties of the hostesses, and also had the job of showing important visitors around the Olympic grounds and buildings.

At the inaugural ceremony of the Munich Olympics it was Silvia who attended to the prominent guests. On the day before the opening she acted as hostess at a reception for VIPs. The Swedish Crown Prince was among the guests and Silvia was delegated to escort him.

Love at first sight

The handsome blond Prince shook hands with Miss Sommerlath and was unable to take his eyes off her for the rest of the evening. 'It just clicked,' he said later.

For Silvia and Carl Gustaf it was love at first sight. They slipped away to secluded clubs in the evenings, where they danced, talked and

fell deeper in love. When Carl Gustaf returned to Stockholm, it was soon obvious to his closest friends that he had lost his heart. He spoke of no one but Silvia and showed no interest at all in nightclubs and parties.

He telephoned Silvia regularly, sometimes calling her several times a day. Silvia visited Stockholm and also met the Prince in other places in Sweden. On these increasingly frequent trips she was put up in the utmost secrecy by close friends of the Prince.

Princess Sibylla dies

The 90th birthday of King Gustaf VI Adolf was celebrated with great pomp and ceremony in the autumn of 1972. The entire Royal Family joined in the festivities, but sadness was to follow. Just a few weeks later, the Crown Prince's mother, Princess Sibylla, died after undergoing a cancer operation. She was only 64.

This was a hard blow for Carl Gustaf, but it was perhaps his grandfather who found it most

♛ *The young Carl Gustaf was as accomplished on skis as he was on the dance-floor. His family had a tradition of spending an annual holiday in the mountains and he liked to return there whenever he could find time* above and right

Popperfoto

Popperfoto

Pressens Bild

difficult to get over Sibylla's death. Since the death of his second wife, Queen Louise, Sibylla had sustained the King and kept him company. The ageing monarch now felt unspeakably lonely, even though Princess Christina and the Crown Prince were still living at the Palace. Carl Gustaf's three eldest sisters had already married and left home.

More and more duties were assumed by the Prince. Despite the fact that he was increasingly busy, he still managed to arrange a number of clandestine meetings with Silvia.

Silvia, meanwhile, had accepted an offer to supervise the training of hostesses for the Winter Olympics at Innsbruck, in Austria. She was appointed Assistant Head of the Protocol Section and would eventually move to Innsbruck.

The secret is out

In the early summer of 1973 Silvia had visited the Prince on the island of Öland. When he stopped at a service station to fill his Porsche, the couple were spotted and were snapped by an alert photographer.

The picture of the dark-haired girl hit the front pages of the newspapers. But nobody knew who she was and several months passed before her identity was revealed. It eventually came out that her name was Silvia and that she lived in Germany. A journalist managed to find her and she did not deny that she was seeing the Swedish Crown Prince. By that time they had known each other for a year.

'It is one thing to like each other,' she said, 'but for that feeling to mature into what is called love takes a long time.'

Silvia had little idea what her discovery by

the Press would entail, but she was soon to learn. The day her name became known she was hounded by reporters, chiefly from the German and Swedish papers. Silvia Sommerlath would never again enjoy anonymity and from now on she was fair game.

The Royal Palace in Stockholm kept the entire affair under wraps. The Court refused to comment but there was much feverish activity behind the scenes. Prince Bertil had already met Silvia Sommerlath, both at the Olympics and on several subsequent occasions. He had been very impressed by the charming young

Svenskt Pressfoto

🔱 *The charming, vivacious teenager from São Paulo had grown in Germany into a radiantly beautiful young woman with a ready smile above who earned her living as an interpreter. When Silvia appeared before the Olympic Organization Committee in 1972, seeking a job at the Munich Olympics, she was picked unhesitatingly for a job as an hostess top*

MUNICH OLYMPICS 1972

Popperfoto

The Olympic Games at Munich were marred by one of the most horrific terrorist attacks ever committed. At dawn on 5 September, a band of Arab guerrillas calling themselves 'Black September' stormed the Israeli building in the Olympic village near Munich. Two athletes were killed and nine taken hostage.

The guerrillas demanded the release of 200 Palestinians held in Israeli jails and a safe passage out of Germany. Following negotiations with the masked terrorists *right*, which were carried out under the personal supervision of the West German Chancellor, Willy Brandt, the terrorists were taken to a military airport from where, it was stated, they would be flown to an Arab country.

A rescue attempt which had been secretly mounted by the German police failed tragically. In a gun battle on the tarmac, all the hostages were killed, as well as four Arabs and one policeman

Allers Photo Press

👑 *Following their meeting in Munich, Carl Gustaf and Silvia kept their relationship secret for almost a year. The first hint the Swedish people had of it was when the Prince stopped for petrol on a visit to Öland and was snapped with Silvia sitting in the passenger seat of his car* left. *The picture's publication caused a mystery; no-one recognized his companion, and there was no comment from the Palace*

girl and wished with all his heart to help the Crown Prince.

Carl Gustaf's sisters also rallied to the cause and a veritable secret organization was set up to help smuggle Silvia in and out of the country and to keep her concealed.

Death of the King

A decisive event took place in September 1973. King Gustaf VI Adolf had been ill during the summer. His condition deteriorated and he died on 15 September at Sofiero, his summer residence.

The Crown Prince, now aged 27, acceded

'Rumours about King Carl Gustaf's impending engagement are considerably exaggerated'

THE PALACE

to the throne as King Carl XVI Gustaf. The day after the death of his grandfather he received the homage of the Swedish people and announced his maxim – 'For Sweden – in keeping with the times.'

The next few months were hectic ones for the young monarch and his private plans had to be postponed. Silvia visited Stockholm in January 1974, in the greatest secrecy. Despite the precautions, the Press discovered that the romance was still on. The Palace was beleaguered by reporters and they also pursued Silvia's parents in Heidelberg and persistently telephoned her brothers and colleagues. All were

pumped for information but nobody revealed anything about the romance.

In January the Court announced that 'rumours about King Carl Gustaf's impending engagement are considerably exaggerated.' At the same time Silvia herself issued a circular to the Press, explaining that she was under contract to the Olympic Committee and intended to work in Innsbruck for the next two years. Neither statement did much to deter the newshounds.

During the summer, the King and Silvia met in both France and Italy. In spite of all the fuss surrounding them, they managed to find secret meeting places where they could spend time together undisturbed.

👑 *In September 1973 Gustaf V died and Carl Gustaf became King. Over the next year or two, his relationship with Silvia was carried on clandestinely; they talked often on the telephone, but could meet only when the demands of their respective lives allowed. As a monarch, Carl Gustaf was sent on a round of official State visits, including one to England in 1975, where he hosted a banquet for Queen Elizabeth II and the Duke of Edinburgh at Claridges* below

Hulton Picture Company

PURSUED BY THE PRESS

In the autumn, Silvia Sommerlath took up her appointment with the Olympic Committee in Innsbruck. Her office was kept under surveillance by the Press. She was forced to live at a secret address and was unable to take a step without attracting attention. Her superiors appealed to the mass media to leave her alone but they were generally ignored. Silvia herself remained quite composed and brushed off every question with a smile.

Her job as Assistant Head of Protocol carried heavy responsibilities. It was a key post in the Olympic organization and Silvia was proud and happy to have been chosen. But the persistent attentions of the media were to change what should have been an open and sociable job into a nerve-racking challenge. That Silvia nevertheless succeeded in carrying out her duties was entirely due to her tough resilience and self-discipline.

The King and Silvia spent Christmas with his sister Desirée and her husband Baron Silfverschiöld at Koberg Palace in western Sweden. New Year was celebrated with the King's sister Birgitta and her husband Prince Johann Georg von Hohenzollern at the ski resort of Klosters, in Switzerland.

Speculation about an engagement and wedding continued, but nothing happened. Silvia spent several weeks in the summer of 1975 with Carl Gustaf at Solliden on the island of Öland. Later that year they cruised in the Mediterranean with friends. Everyone waited for a communiqué but the Court denied all knowledge of the King's future plans with regard to marriage.

'This utterly intolerable situation is quite alien to my nature,' said Silvia. 'I wish for nothing more than for it to end.'

Thinking it over

Carl Gustaf and Silvia were, of course, deeply in love. The romance which began with love at first sight had turned into a serious relationship. But even so they hesitated before making the final decision.

There were no longer any formal obstacles to the marriage. As Crown Prince, Carl Gustaf had needed the permission of the King, but now that he himself was King he was free to marry whomever he wished.

When answering the eternal question ab-

♛ *King Carl XVI Gustaf was acclaimed on his accession while surrounded on the balcony of the Royal Palace at Stockholm by the rest of the Royal Family* top, left to right *Princess Christina, Princess Désirée, Carl Gustaf, Princess Birgitta, Princess Margaretha and Prince Bertil. The Princesses wore mourning clothes in memory of their grandfather*

♛ *Like Carl Gustaf, Silvia enjoyed winter sports. In 1975 she was spotted at the Swiss ski resort of Klosters* below left *at the same time as the King was enjoying a holiday there. Though they were not seen together in public, the 'coincidence' reawakened Press speculation about the relationship. A year later* below, *Silvia was working at the Winter Olympics in Innsbruck, still denying that she and King Carl Gustaf had any plans to marry*

One thing which worried the King and his family was Silvia's nationality. The difficulty Sibylla had experienced, on account of her German origin, was still fresh in their minds, and they were afraid that history would repeat itself. They were also aware that in conservative quarters it was thought that a Queen should be of Royal descent.

No skeletons

Needless to say, Silvia's background was discreetly checked. The Palace wanted no skeletons in the cupboard. Strange as it may seem, there was nothing derogatory to be said about her, and not the slightest little fault could be found. The German gutter Press was equally unable to unearth anything remarkable.

Silvia was indeed perfect – an intelligent, beautiful and unusually charming woman, with a rare radiance, a sincere concern for people and admirable self-discipline. In addition, she had a good sense of humour, and a warm nature. She was also considerate, loyal, reliable and honest.

Everyone who met her kept their fingers crossed, in the hope that the King would propose and that Silvia would say 'Yes'.

The engagement

At long last, the engagement was announced on 12 March 1976. The following day, the newly-engaged couple held a Press conference, attended by battalions of TV, radio and newspaper reporters and cameramen.

In a television interview, the King said the romance had clicked from the first meeting and had been clicking ever since. Silvia showed off her engagement ring of white gold with a large diamond. It had belonged, she said, to Sibylla. Asked whether she had any particular Queen as an ideal, she immediately replied, 'No, but I have a King.'

The following day's papers said, 'She came, she saw, she conquered.' The people of Sweden took to Silvia immediately. For them, too, it was love at first sight.

out his marriage he replied, 'We are still hesitant about taking the step. Because of my special position I must consider such a matter more carefully than most people. In fact, it isn't enough to consider it once or twice, I must do it several times.'

Silvia later spoke of her own thoughts and feelings at the time. 'I searched myself thoroughly – really thought things over in great depth. But of course I was quite unable to imagine what being a Queen would entail. I don't suppose anyone can.'

What bothered Silvia most was the knowledge that royalty cannot have the same kind of private life as ordinary people. During the last couple of years, she had come to know what it was like to be watched, guarded, photographed and scrutinized in the minutest detail. It was not a pleasant experience for a person who, until then, had led a perfectly normal life.

👑 *The engagement of King Carl XVI Gustaf and Miss Silvia Sommerlath was formally announced on 12 March 1976 top picture. A celebratory dinner at the Royal Palace six days later was Silvia's first official occasion above. A much less formal celebration took place at the Villa Beylon, home of the King's sister, Princess Christina and her husband Tord Magnuson, where both families gathered right. Mrs Sommerlath stands next to her daughter, while her father is on the extreme left*

Syndication International

Hulton Picture Company

Pressens Bild

DROTTNINGHOLM

Drottningholm Palace, the current Royal home, is often called 'the Versailles of the North'. Much of its inspiration certainly is French – the gardens, for instance, were laid out along the lines of those by Le Nôtre, Louis XIV's designer at Versailles – but there is also a distinct Nordic country-house feel to it. Started in 1662, its architect was the Swede Nicodemus Tessin the Elder, who was succeeded by his son; further wings were added in 1774. Once used only as a summer Palace, it is built on an island in Lake Malar

Svenskt Pressfoto

Robert Harding

Pressens Bild

♕ The imposing stairwell *left* provides a fine classical entrance. Marble pillars, wall fascia and balusters are set off by statues of Apollo and the Muses beneath an allegorical painted ceiling

Pressens Bild

👑 The coolly rigid exterior of the Palace *above*, with its formal gardens in the style of Le Nôtre, conceals perhaps unexpected lavishness inside. The gilded Riks Hall (State Hall) *right* was restored by the King's great-great-grandfather, Oskar I. The theatre *below*, in the grounds, dates from 1766 and is a perfect home for Baroque opera. It lay unused for 100 years until the cobwebs were dusted away

👑 The Queen Room *above* has a fine collection of portraits of European Queens. The room is in 18th-century Empire style

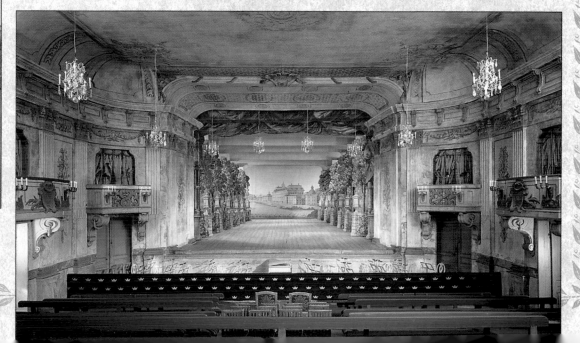

Drottingholms Teatermuseum

A JOYOUS OCCASION

THE WEDDING DAY WAS A TRIUMPH, ENJOYED BY VIPs AND THE PEOPLE. SWEDEN FELL FOR THEIR NEW QUEEN, WHO SEEMED TAILOR-MADE FOR THE ROLE

THE FOUR-YEAR ROMANCE WAS TO END exactly as in a fairy tale. The woman of the people would get her Prince – or rather her King.

A tremendous wedding was now planned. At the express wish of King Carl Gustaf, it was to be an unforgettable festival for royalty and ordinary people alike.

In consultation with Carl Gustaf and Silvia, the Royal Palace arranged the pageant down to the last detail. Choirs and orchestras all over the country started practising. Menus for lunches, receptions and dinners were compiled. Invitations were sent out, uniforms were brushed and checked, harnesses and carriage fittings were polished and horses were groomed in readiness for the big day.

The happy couple, relaxed throughout the ceremony, walk hand in hand down the aisle below and below right, taking with them the good wishes of family, friends and heads of state. The scene inside the 300-year-old Storkyrkan (the Grand Church) was one of grandeur enlivened by dazzling floral arrangements and the colourful finery of the congregation. Beside the altar are the crowns of Lovisa Ulrika, who was crowned in 1751, and (on the right) Erik XIV, who became King of Sweden in 1561

Stockholm was spruced up and decked out with flowers, flags and portraits of the engaged couple. These were hectic days for the lovers. Telegrams and wedding presents poured into the Palace and guests started arriving.

Happy parents

Walther and Alice Sommerlath were overjoyed that their daughter had finally won the man she loved. Silvia's parents had had to console her many times when things looked black. In their heart of hearts they had believed that the romance would not have a happy ending. They could never imagine that their own little 'Kitten' would become the Queen of Sweden.

By tradition it is the bride's father who makes the wedding speech. Of all those in-

Pressens Bild

volved in the wedding, Walther Sommerlath was perhaps the most nervous. 'I went around thinking that I, Walther Sommerlath, was to stand before royalty and presidents and make a speech, and I found it difficult to sleep the night before the wedding,' Mr. Sommerlath confessed afterwards.

Pre-nuptial celebrations

Festivities commenced on the eve of the wedding when the City of Stockholm invited the King and Silvia and 350 guests to a buffet luncheon in the grounds of the Town Hall. Mem-

'*I found it difficult to sleep the night before the wedding*'

THE BRIDE'S FATHER

bers of the Government and Parliament paid their respects by arranging a gala concert at the Stockholm Opera House in the evening. Among the performers were well-known Swedish artistes, including opera singer Birgit Nilsson and the ABBA pop group.

For the concert Silvia wore a Royal coronet for the first time, and a fabulous white gown strewn with sparkling beads. The gown had been designed by Marc Bohan of Dior and achieved just the right effect. A shimmering fairy-tale Princess entered the Royal box at the Opera House and she was greeted by enthusias-

tic applause from the audience.

After the gala concert, the King invited his guests to a ball at Drottningholm Palace. The engaged couple opened the ball to the lilting strains of an imperial waltz and the party continued until sunrise.

A Royal gathering

On the day of the wedding, 19 June 1976, expectant onlookers thronged the streets from daybreak. A feeling of joy and expectation was in the air that sunny day. Invited guests waited in Storkyrkan, the Stockholm Cathedral.

Svenskt Pressfoto

♛ *Emerging from the Cathedral above Queen Silvia and Carl Gustaf were greeted by thousands of wellwishers. As they stood and waved to the crowd they made a radiant couple and were obviously delighted by the reception they received*

♛ *Outside the Cathedral the scene was one of calmly ordered pomp and circumstance. A parade of Royal guardsmen, wearing black bearskins with white plumes, neatly complemented the black and white of the Royal carriage and the clothes of the Royal couple themselves. As always in these situations it required the combined efforts of several people to manoeuvre the long bridal train into the carriage. Everything passed off without the slightest hitch*

Hulton Picture Company

♛ *The drive from the Cathedral epitomized the happy informality of the day. Seated in an open carriage on a fine, sunny afternoon, Silvia and Carl Gustaf were showered with rice and confetti as they drove slowly through the good-humoured crowd. They took it all in good part and seemed to enjoy it quite as much as the tens of thousands of spectators who had been camped out for hours to secure the best places*

Pressens Bild

♛ *The horse-drawn carriage took the newlyweds to the island of Skeppsholmen where the Royal barge* Vasaorden *awaited them. Freshly painted in blue, white and gold, the barge had a richly carved crown atop the cabin. Swedish flags fluttered from stem and stern*

Among the distinguished gathering were the crowned heads of all the neighbouring European countries: Queen Margrethe of Denmark and her husband Prince Henrik, King Olav of Norway, Queen Fabiola and King Baudouin of Belgium and the Grand Duke and Duchess of Luxembourg.

A murmur went through the assembled throng when the bride arrived. She looked ra-

diantly beautiful in her white silk Dior gown. The bridal crown of red gold and cameos had once belonged to Queen Josephine, and the long rustling train of Brussels lace had previously been worn by the King's sisters. The bridal bouquet was composed of jasmine blossoms, white orchids and lily of the valley. The pages and bridesmaids were the children of Silvia's brothers and the King's sisters.

A fairy-tale wedding

The King met his bride at the entrance to the Cathedral and gave her a tender kiss on the cheek before they proceeded up the aisle.

'It was a wonderful day for me and my wife'

CARL GUSTAF

Neither of them showed the slightest nervousness, and they smilingly acknowledged relatives and friends as they walked to the altar.

The wedding was seen on television by 200 million people around the world. At home in Germany, Silvia's former schoolfriends from Luisenschule no doubt watched the historic ceremony with special interest.

Archbishop Olof Sundby officiated and Silvia's uncle, Professor Ernst Sommerlath, D.D., recited the lines of 'The Lord is my Shepherd'.

At 12.21 the King slipped the ring on his wife's finger and Sweden had a Queen. A tear of

Svenskt Pressfoto

joy could be seen on the bride's cheek and Silvia's parents wept with happiness. 'It was just as unreal as a fairy tale,' said Walther Sommerlath afterwards.

Procession to the Palace

The Royal couple rode in an open carriage through the streets of central Stockholm. The pavements were lined with 180,000 people, who waved their flags and flowers and showered the wedding couple with rice.

The procession made its way to the island of Skeppsholmen opposite the Royal Palace. *Vasaorden*, a gilded barge, was waiting at the island, with a crew of 18 cadets. They rowed the newlyweds across the channel, while ships of the Swedish Coastal Fleet and Danish and British warships fired salutes. When the barge arrived at the Palace landing stage a cheer went up, and 150 musicians in traditional costume struck up the bridal march as the newlyweds walked along the red carpet towards their new home, the Royal Palace.

'It was a wonderful day for me and my wife. Thank you all for coming and making this a memorable and joyous occasion. We are very happy,' said the King, in his speech to the people of Sweden.

Camera Press

🜲 *From the first, the Queen was immensely popular with the Swedish people. She often wears the local costume above of the region she is visiting and invariably seems as pleased to be there as are the crowds who turn up to see her and Carl Gustaf*

🜲 *In October 1976, just a few months after the wedding, the notable Swedish photographer, Lennart Nilsson, took this official portrait left of Her Majesty. For the occasion she wore a parure that had belonged to Joséphine de Beauharnais, who became Queen of Sweden on her marriage to King Oskar I in 1823*

When asked by the Press how she saw her future role, Queen Silvia replied: 'I want to try to be of help.'

A sensible and unassuming reply. Neither Silvia nor anyone else is able exactly to describe what being a Queen involves. It is quite simply the kind of job that is what one makes of it, as other crowned Queens would confirm.

Well qualified

It so happened that Silvia had a virtually perfect background for the job. With her long experience of representational duties, she was accustomed to organizing people and events and to meeting all kinds of people. She also had appropriate personal qualities, including self-discipline, stamina, intelligence and humour.

But Silvia had to take the step from a normal middle-class life to one where her daily routine was regulated by the written and unwritten rules of the Court. Even though Sweden is a modern monarchy it cannot be said that the Royal couple live like ordinary people. They are surrounded by adjutants, servants, security guards, ladies-in-waiting and other staff. There is not much room or opportunity for a private life.

The King was born to that life and trained for his duties; the Queen had to learn as she went along. Moreover, she had to learn Swedish, as well as much about her new country's history, culture, politics and customs.

Loved by the people

Right from the outset Silvia was received with almost south European warmth by the Swedes, who generally regard themselves as stiff, shy and reserved. Great crowds cheered her and they practically deluged her with flowers wherever she appeared.

The Queen quickly became the country's most popular figure and the King had to come to terms with being overshadowed by his wife. Invitations poured into the Palace – everyone wanted the Royal couple to visit them.

It is customary in Sweden for the King to acquaint himself with all parts of his country. This Royal progress is known as an *Eriksgata* and is done by stages, as Sweden is a fairly large country. Towns and districts scheduled for a visit need time to prepare.

The tours made by the Royal couple have been veritable triumphal processions.

The Queen talked enthusiastically about her experiences travelling around the country: 'It is hard to describe the rapport between us and the people we meet. Perhaps this is the same kind of response a musician can get from his audience. It is a sort of mutual expression of confidence – a warmth which I regard as an acknowledgement.'

At the wedding lunch, Prince Bertil welcomed Silvia as the country's Queen and as a new member of the family. And just before Walther Sommerlath rose to make his speech, he was handed a note from his daughter. It read, 'I love you, daddy. Your Kitten.'

Very much in love

The official part of the wedding was over and the families' private celebrations could begin. Amid all the Royal splendour and festivities there were two people who had been joined in love. The aura of happiness surrounding the wedding couple was plain for all to see.

The following day, the newly-married couple left in the utmost secrecy for their honeymoon in Hawaii and Africa. They were at last free to enjoy each other's company without anxiety. They could now begin in peace and quiet to plan their life together as man and wife and as King and Queen.

WORKING TOGETHER

It was a pleasure for Carl Gustaf to have someone with whom to share his work and his weekdays. He had been quite lonely since the death of his mother, and he grew even more isolated when he became King. But he now had his wife Silvia. They could discuss the day's events, talk about people they had met and make plans together.

The King's aunt, Queen Ingrid of Denmark, took Silvia under her wing. She taught her a thousand and one things a Queen should know. Trivial things such as how to secure her hat in a high wind, how to dress for different occasions and how to run a Royal household. She also gave Silvia an insight into a Queen's official life and duties, and the confidence with which to meet her new responsibilities.

'From the start, Queen Ingrid advised me to be myself,' Silvia later said. 'I know now from personal experience that this is the only way to cope with this job. One must give of oneself. But to do that one must know oneself.'

Setting up home

The Royal couple moved into a private apartment in the Palace. Their offices, too, were situated in the Palace.

The Royal Palace is owned by the State, not by the King. The private apartment, however, was furnished by the King and Queen themselves. They chose a blend of modern pieces and inherited antiques. The Royal couple's apartment consists of about ten rooms.

The King said jokingly at the engagement ceremony that Silvia had still not seen all over the Palace. This was, in fact, probably true, as the Stockholm Royal Palace has 608 rooms and is the world's largest occupied Palace. About 150 people work in it.

Camera Press

The Palace was rebuilt after a fire in 1697 and the work took 60 years to complete. The earliest parts are furnished in the Baroque fashion but, for the most part, the Palace is in the Rococo style. The 11 Royal couples who have lived in the Palace, however, have all left their mark on it.

For the Queen, who grew up in a fairly modest house, it must have been a major adjustment to move into a 600-room Palace. To

♛ *Wonderful though the wedding day had been, the Royal couple must have relished a few quiet moments to themselves after all the pageantry. Their faithful companion at moments like this was Charlie the Labrador, a present from Silvia to Carl Gustaf*

♛ *In the autumn of 1976 the King and Queen paid a State visit to Holland. Their trip was a great success and they were made very welcome by Queen Juliana and Prince Bernhard (seated). Also present were Crown Princess Beatrix and Prince Claus von Amsberg (standing right) who had both been honoured guests at the Stockholm wedding*

Allers Photo Press

Swedish Tourist Board

THE ROYAL PALACE, STOCKHOLM

The largest of the Scandinavian Palaces, the Royal Palace *above* in Stockholm is a massive Baroque building facing the waterside. It was built on the site of the old Three Crowns Palace which was burnt down in May 1697. The very next day the architect Nicodemus Tessin the Younger came up with a plan for a new Palace (indeed, he was the focus of rumours that suggested that the fire was not entirely accidental) and soon set to work on it, employing a team of French artists and craftsmen to decorate the interior. The work was completed by his son Carl Gustaf after an 18-year break (due to Sweden's bankruptcy). The Palace has some 608 rooms and is famous for its Boucher tapestries, Savonnerie carpets, French furniture and *objets d'art*. One of its most appealing rooms is King Oskar II's writing room *right*, which has been kept exactly as he left it when he died in 1907. It is a comfortable room, full of family photographs and other mementoes

Svenskt Pressfoto

get to her own apartment she had to pass a long row of locked doors and armed guards. In a way, though, it must have been a relief for her to feel protected after being hounded and harassed for several years. Her private life had been scrutinized in great detail, but now, at last, she had a degree of secure privacy.

Private and public lives

The Royal couple were careful to keep their official and private lives quite separate, right from the start. The moments when they can relax and be themselves are extremely precious.

Both of them are outgoing, sociable people and they often enjoy the company of their many mutual friends. Naturally, most of them are friends of the King, whom Silvia got to know during her long romance with the then Crown Prince.

Just three months after the wedding the Royal couple travelled to Holland on their first State visit. Beautiful, smiling and completely at ease, Silvia passed the test with flying colours and was congratulated by Queen Juliana.

Lynne Robinson

STYLE ON A BUDGET

Unlike many female Royals, Queen Silvia does not have a lot of money to spend on clothes so, although her wardrobe is stylish and varied, it tends to be practical rather than highly fashionable. She does not, as a rule, use top international designers but local makers who recognize her need for 'mix and match' outfits

Brussels lace veil and cameo tiara are Royal heirlooms. Veil has a shoulder length flounce at the back

Bouquet of jasmine blossoms, white orchids and lily-of-the-valley

Princess line silk-satin bridal gown, with raised edge seams around neck-line, shoulder and side-front dress seams

♛ For her wedding gown *left*, Silvia did choose a top designer, Christian Dior. The princess-line dress in white silk is remarkably simple and elegant with a long silk train falling from the shoulders. Her veil of Brussels lace had previously been worn by the King's sisters

Reginald Davis

♛ Silvia *above* often chooses white or cream for formal occasions, colours which set off her dark, glossy hair and exotic beauty to good effect

Self-fabric bow trim on shoulder line

Single-shouldered sleeveless taffeta evening dress, with gathered and draped dropped waist bodice

Popperfoto

♛ Despite a skiing accident, Sylvia looks particularly chic *above* during a visit with the King to Paris in May 1990

Full, gathered bell-shaped, floor length skirt

Outfit worn with a white frilled edge evening wrap

♛ This dazzling blue taffeta gown *left* was worn by the Queen to a grand gala performance at Carnegie Hall during the state visit to the US in 1988. A practical instance of Silvia's thrift with clothes is that she also wore this gown to the 50th birthday party for King Constantine of Greece in 1990

HEIRS AND PLACES

A BABY PRINCESS WAS SOON TO BE JOINED BY A BROTHER AND A SISTER. THE GROWING FAMILY MOVED TO A COUNTRY PALACE AND A BUSY ROUND OF FAMILY COMMITMENTS AND PUBLIC DUTIES

Reginald Davis

A T THE END OF 1976 THE COURT announced that the Queen was expecting a child. The news was greeted with delight by the Swedish people. Despite the pregnancy, Silvia went ahead with a planned State visit to Belgium in the spring. The Queen won everyone's sympathy when she saw the tiring programme through, without showing the fatigue she felt.

Queen Silvia gave birth to a daughter on 14 July 1977. At an extra Cabinet meeting the King announced that the girl would be named Victoria Alice Desirée.

Victoria's birth gave rise to a debate concerning the order of succession. Parliament decided to change the law to enable the first-born child to succeed to the throne. This meant that for the first time ever Sweden had a future Queen. Previously only males could become monarchs.

'Giving birth to a child is the most wonderful experience of all,' said the radiantly happy mother when the new Princess, only 18 days old, was presented to the Press. From then on it was the proud father who took most pictures of the baby.

The family enjoyed the whole summer on

⚜ In the spring of 1976 the King and Queen undertook a State visit to Belgium. Silvia was pregnant with her first child but never flagged for a moment. They are seen above with the Mayor of Brussels and his wife

'Giving birth to a child is the most wonderful experience of all'

SILVIA

the island of Öland and in the autumn Victoria was ceremonially christened. Her godparents were Crown Prince Harald of Norway, the then Crown Princess Beatrix of Holland, the King's sister Désirée and the Queen's brother Ralf Sommerlath.

Victoria was a captivatingly sweet child, with her mother's brown eyes and her father's sense of humour. The parents were fully agreed that their child should receive a modern upbringing and, as far as possible, attend ordinary schools. They both came from large families and hoped that Victoria, too, would soon have brothers and sisters.

Birth of a Prince
In May 1979 Victoria was joined by a brother. He was named Carl Philip Edmund Bertil. In the spring of that year the Royal couple had made a highly successful State visit to West Germany, the Queen's homeland. It caused tremendous excitement and was almost too much for Silvia, who was in the seventh month of her pregnancy. There were daily television reports and wherever the Royal couple went they were met by enormous crowds of people, all anxious to catch a glimpse of 'their' Queen.

SOLLIDEN

Solliden *above*, the summer Palace on the Baltic island of Öland, was built in 1903 for Queen Viktoria, wife of Gustaf V, who loved the healthy climate and unique wildlife of the island. King Carl Gustaf shares her passion for the place: 'It is fragrant. You can feel the wind and hear the swallows overhead.'

The building has three stories; the main living quarters, including a grand entrance hall, are on the first floor, as is Queen Viktoria's study and the loggia, an Italianate verandah with a view south over the Strait of Kalmar. A flight of stairs leads down through a pergola to the grounds, which contain woodlands, pastures, orchards and gardens landscaped in Italian and English styles

That year the Royal couple looked forward eagerly to spending their summer at Solliden. At this quiet retreat the King and Queen were able to devote themselves fully to two-year-old Victoria and her newborn brother.

The family retreat

The Royal Family are entirely private when they live at Solliden. They swim in the secluded bay, take trips in their boat, fish and play with the children. Silvia's parents visit them once a year and so do the Royal children's cousins.

The Royal couple do their own shopping in the little town of Borgholm and the King frequently prepares the food himself. He is a skilful cook, and on Öland he is especially fond of preparing dinner from fish he himself has smoked and cured. With this he will serve vegetables grown in the garden of Solliden. In the autumn the whole family helps pick fruit and berries to preserve or freeze, for use in the winter. The Queen is particularly fond of asparagus, which is nowadays grown very successfully at Solliden.

A number of animals are kept at Solliden for the children's sake. For many years Charlie the labrador was the family pet. He was a gift to

♔ *Princess Victoria, in the arms of her father* above, *became the heir to the throne after a change in the law*

♔ *The State visit to West Germany* below *created tremendous excitement, with crowds flocking to see the Queen*

35

the King from Silvia, long before they were married. Charlie was also the favourite of the Press photographers. He thoroughly enjoyed being in the limelight and always wanted to be in the front row. Charlie died eventually and he has been succeeded by another labrador.

Moving to another Palace

Many generations of Swedish Kings have lived at the Stockholm Royal Palace. None of them had small children, however. As Victoria and Carl Philip began to grow up, their parents felt they should get away from traffic noise and exhaust fumes to a place where the children could play outdoors. They decided to move to one of the other Palaces.

They chose Drottningholm, a magnificent Palace just outside Stockholm, on the shores of Lake Mälaren. Drottningholm is known as the Versailles of Stockholm because it resembles the French Palace in style and has similar landscaped gardens. The present Palace was rebuilt after a fire in the middle of the 17th century.

Over the years Drottningholm has fre-

Pressens Bild

Pressens Bild

☙ *With a helping hand from Carl Gustaf, Silvia* above *weighs a fish she has caught. She has learnt to share her husband's enthusiasm for this restful sport*

☙ *Much to Silvia's amusement, Princess Victoria and baby Carl Philip 'feed' a sculptured deer* below *in the grounds of Solliden, the family's summer retreat*

☙ *Princess Victoria and Charlie the Labrador were irresistibly photogenic. This delightful picture* above *was taken on Victoria's first birthday by Carl Gustaf, who regularly snaps informal shots of the family*

Hulton Picture Company

Pressens Bild

quently been used as a dowager's home by widowed Queens. Until the present century, however, when central heating was installed, it was exclusively a summer residence. It was Gustaf V, the King's great-grandfather, who broke with tradition. In the early 1900s he began the practice of celebrating Christmas at Drottningholm. Each year he would be joined there by the entire Royal Family.

Part of the 300-year-old Palace was to be converted into a private apartment for the present Royal Family. A comfortable home was arranged and furnished in the south wing, where the enclosed courtyard became a sheltered playground for the children. The King and Queen took an active interest in planning their home and chose the wallcoverings, furniture and colour schemes for the 20 or so rooms in the apartment. The furnishings are of the light and cheerful kind that children like and the furniture itself is robust and play-proof.

Princess Madeleine

In 1982, one year after moving in, Princess Madeleine was born. She was the first child to see the light of day at Drottningholm since Gustaf V was born there in 1858. The King, who had attended fathers' training courses, was present at the entire birth for the first time.

Just like her brother and sister, the new baby was christened in Stockholm Cathedral by the Archbishop. She was named Madeleine Thérèse Amelie Josephine. Her godparents were the Queen's brother Walther Sommerlath, Princess Benedikte of Denmark, the King's youngest sister, Princess Christina, and Prince Andreas von Sachsen, Coburg und Gotha, who is a cousin of the King.

Active parents

All three children were born in the early summer and spent the first few months of their lives at Solliden. The summer of 1982 gave Victoria and Carl Philip a chance to get to know their new little sister, as they helped to rock her cradle. Never before had the King shown as much interest in any of his newborn children as he did in Madeleine. Perhaps this was because he witnessed the birth from start to finish and experienced that great moment when the child first cried. He later referred to it as an utterly marvellous experience and one which he wished all fathers might have.

The Queen has breast-fed all three children and has nursed them herself as far as possible. They all slept by her bed for the first six months so that she could pacify them if they woke. Silvia has read widely on the subject of child psychology and is aware of the importance of security and parental contact in a child's early years.

The King has always been very fond of chil-

The Royal Family above have found a summer paradise at Solliden on the island of Öland. The arrival of Princess Madeleine – just one-year-old here – completed the family

dren and he assumed the role of father with tremendous zeal. He thoroughly enjoys playing and romping with the children and has taught them how to swim and how to fish. At weekends, when the Royal couple are without servants, it is the King who cooks the food and the Queen who does the washing up. The children are always in the kitchen and are allowed to lend a hand.

Like most youngsters the Royal children are mad about spaghetti, and they frequently have home-made pasta which the King makes in his own pasta machine. The whole family takes part in preparing for Christmas. They dip candles, make sausages and bake ginger biscuits, just like any other Swedish family.

Life at Drottningholm

At Drottningholm the children have been able to lead a fairly normal life. Like other young children they enjoy the delights of the garden swing or playing in their sand-box. They feed geese and ducks at the water's edge, and have learned to cycle on the gravel paths. In winter, they go tobogganing.

Because the Royal couple have irregular

Svenskt Pressfoto

Svenskt Pressfoto

👑 *In their different ways the Royal couple and the pop group ABBA have been popular ambassadors for Sweden. ABBA performed at the gala concert on the eve of the wedding and have met the King and Queen at many events since* above

👑 *On the State visit to the Soviet Union in 1978* left *Silvia was shown around a Russian Orthodox seminary in the city of Zagorsk, to the north of Moscow*

working hours and often have to travel, there are three nannies who look after the children in shifts. The private household has a staff of about ten. In addition to the nannies, the couple have a chef and two butlers who wait on table and attend to other household duties. A valet and a lady-in-waiting look after the Royal couple's wardrobes, and two servants clean the apartment and the rest of the Palace. There is also a chauffeur for official occasions.

The move to Drottningholm has meant that the Royal couple have found it easier to keep their work and leisure separate. The King nowadays drives his BMW to his office in the Stockholm Royal Palace every morning. The Queen's working days were shorter when the children were small, but she is now often in her office at the same time as her husband.

Royal duties and interests

Only personal friends of the Royal couple are invited to Drottningholm. All State receptions are held at the Royal Palace. Along with the White House in Washington, however, Drottningholm is probably the only Head of State's dwelling that is open to the general public. The Baroque gardens and English Park are also popular with visitors.

But it is, perhaps, the 18th-century theatre that has made Drottningholm most famous. It is one of the few theatres in the world from that era that has been preserved completely intact. Operas are still performed there in the light of flickering wax candles.

The Royal couple have a heavy workload. They both take their duties seriously and their days — save for holidays — are carefully planned, occasionally up to a year ahead.

It is said that all male Bernadottes mature late, and Carl Gustaf was certainly somewhat immature when he became King. He was unsure of himself and was often shy at official functions. Sometimes, too, he gave the impression of being sullen. In time, however, he has grown accustomed to his job and is now much more relaxed. He is fond of joking when protocol allows. He has also learnt to laugh at his mistakes and he finds it much easier nowadays to chat to strangers.

Carl Gustaf dislikes being idle. A full programme is what he likes best, and he prefers events to move fast without any dead spots. Some of those who work with him are elderly men and, not being as fit as the King, they sometimes have difficulty keeping up with him.

The King has a genuine interest in the countryside and the environment. He is President of the Swedish section of the World Wide

♛ *Japan proved a challenge to the King and Queen in many ways. The language and culture were completely different but they were warmly welcomed as ever. Silvia, under the eye of keen tutors, tries her hand above at flower arranging in the traditional Japanese style*

NOBEL PRIZE

Each year Carl Gustaf and Queen Silvia officiate at Stockholm's Nobel Prize Ceremony *right*. This prestigious event was founded by one of Sweden's most famous and richest citizens, Alfred Nobel, an armaments manufacturer who died in 1896. Not only was Nobel the inventor of dynamite but he also set up the industrial complex at Bofors in Sweden which even today produces a substantial amount of the world's weaponry. It is ironic that this great philanthropist apparently saw no wrong in profiting from the fortunes of war. A year before his death, he signed a will which, in less than 300 words, stipulated that the proceeds of his wealth were to be used for annual prizes in five categories: physics, chemistry, physiology or medicine, literature and – the best known of all – the promotion of peace.

Fund for Nature (WWF) and is actively involved in its work. As a modern monarch he also regards it as part of his job to promote Swedish trade and industry abroad. He is more interested in engineering and industry than in cultural matters.

Silvia is at least as ambitious as her husband. To ensure maximum efficiency they

👑 *Protocol was observed to the letter for the State visit of Queen Elizabeth II and Prince Philip right. Carl Gustaf, in full admiral's uniform like Philip, took the salute when the guard of honour welcomed the British couple at the airport*

Svenskt Pressfoto

LAPPLAND

Erhan Güner

Lappland, Sweden's largest and most northerly province, is regularly visited by King Carl Gustaf and Queen Silvia *above*. This is the home of Scandinavia's second race, the Lapps or Samer, who for centuries followed a nomadic existence with their reindeer herds in the lands which now make up Finland, Norway and the USSR, as well as Sweden. Traditionally, the Lapps have their own language, religion, dress and customs, although much has been eroded by 20th-century civilization. The Lapps, however, still depend for their existence on their reindeer herds. Nowadays, only the men care for the animals and follow the herd to the mountains during the summer months; they use helicopters, motorbikes and walkie-talkies to help them and to keep in touch with their families in the towns and villages. The reindeer are driven down the mountains in autumn and are then slaughtered for their meat, which is considered a great delicacy

nowadays often split up and take on separate tasks. Silvia is more intimately involved in social questions, especially those concerning children and young people. She is also very interested in art and music.

An open-ended job

'We try not only to *do* our best,' Silvia once said, 'we also try to *give* our best. Being a Queen carries a lot of responsibilities, and it is difficult to say exactly what the job involves. In most jobs it is possible to attain tangible results, but that is not so in my case. There is no beginning and no end.'

In the 14 years of their marriage the Royal couple have made innumerable State visits and have received just as many. The most exciting foreign journeys were no doubt those to the Soviet Union and Japan, while the visit to Sweden that drew most attention was that of Queen Elizabeth II of England.

The Royal couple have sometimes been asked what occupations they would have chosen if they were not royalty. Carl Gustaf has always asserted that he would have turned his hand to farming, while Silvia would have devoted herself to helping handicapped children.

Camera Press

But both emphasize that they enjoy the work they are doing at present.

King Carl Gustaf must be one of the world's poorest monarchs. His annual civil list grant remained unchanged from the day he became King, in 1973, until 1990, when he was voted an increase.

The money voted to the Royal Family is supposed to be sufficient to pay a staff of 65, and to keep the Royal Palaces in good repair, defray all representational expenses and cover

'Being a Queen carries a lot of responsibilities.... There is no beginning and no end'

SILVIA

the costs of all official journeys and events. The King does not receive a special salary and neither his wife nor children receive personal money grants.

When all expenses have been paid, the King is allowed to keep any surplus. To date that has not been sufficient to cover the family's private expenses. These, of course, have increased in step with the growing family and with inflation.

The King's personal fortune is in the region of £7 million, a fairly modest one compared to those of the English and Dutch royalty.

He owns no Palaces, but he does own the

palatial Solliden, as well as a holiday house in the mountains and a small fishing lodge in the far north of the country. Most of the Queen's jewellery is the property of the State. So, too, is the Royal aircraft, which is occasionally used by government officials, and the Royal train.

The Royal family pay their servants themselves, in the same way as they pay for all private travel, clothing, food and cars not used for official purposes. Their homes are furnished with inherited furniture and with pieces they themselves have bought.

Waste not, want not

It is well known that Carl Gustaf and Silvia are extremely economical. The Queen wears the same gowns many times. She favours dresses which can easily be altered and two-piece outfits, so that the skirt and blouse can be worn separately. When a dress goes out of fashion, a seamstress will use the cloth to make the Queen a new garment.

The Royal Family make use of everything grown at Solliden and Drottningholm. The King is an expert and frequent hunter and what he bags inevitably finds its way into the deep-freeze chests at Drottningholm. It is not unusual for guests at official dinners to be served roe deer or elk shot by the King, accompanied by vegetables and berries picked by the family in their garden at Solliden.

The Royal couple always plan their menus themselves, whether they are for a Nobel Prize-giving banquet or a simple dinner with the children. As they are invited to several elegant dinner parties a week, at which they are served sole, salmon and paté de foie gras, they prefer to eat simple fare at other times. Sausages and meatballs are often served at the Royal table.

♛ *Carl Gustaf's attempts at making Christmas decorations above are unlikely to win him any prizes – but they do provide the rest of the family with a lot of harmless amusement*

Swedish Tourist Board

♛ *Much of the Queen's time – time she might prefer to spend with the family – is taken up with State duties, but she always performs these with a smile*

FAMILY MATTERS

The great blessing of Silvia and Carl Gustaf's marriage has been their three lively, handsome children. Every moment of their growing-up has been lovingly documented, and the King himself, a keen amateur photographer, has taken many fine portraits of them, capturing the intimate family moments of one of Europe's most accessible Royal Families

♛ In 1988, Victoria, Carl Philip and Madeleine were photographed *right* wearing floral coronets as part of the midsummer festivities at Solliden on the island of Öland

♛ Crown Princess Victoria celebrated her first birthday on 14 July 1978. To mark the occasion, her father took a series of photographs of her with her king-size teddy bear *left*. Summers in Öland always provided good photographic opportunities. Two-year-old Prince Carl Philip helped his father steer, in a family portrait taken in 1981 *below left*

Pressens Bild

♛ The couple's youngest child, Princess Madeleine, is the mischievous scamp of the family, forever getting into scrapes. This rare shot of her looking winsome and cradling a young rabbit *above* was taken at Solliden in 1986, when she was four years old

Pressens Bild

GROWING TOGETHER

HOLIDAYS WITH FAMILY AND FRIENDS FIT IN WITH OFFICIAL ENGAGEMENTS AND SCHOOL TERMS. THE YOUNG ROYALS HAVE DIFFERENT CHARACTERS, WHILE THE ROYAL MARRIAGE HAS BECOME A WARM RELATIONSHIP

T HE ROYAL COUPLE ARE BOTH FOND OF sports and love the outdoor life. They enjoy themselves most of all when they are skiing or sailing. They always treat themselves to a couple of holidays abroad with the children each year, one of them in Switzerland or Austria, the other in some tropical paradise where they can swim and sunbathe. Easter is always spent in their mountain chalet in Storlien and during the summer they stay at Solliden.

When time permits the Queen will take a few days off to visit her parents in Heidelberg or to see her brothers, one of whom lives in Paris and the other in Brussels.

The King's eldest sister, Margaretha, is married to John Ambler and lives in England. Their contact with Sweden is slight, although John usually visits Sweden with his wife in the autumn to take part in an elk shoot. Princess Birgitta lives in Munich and meets her brother and sister-in-law much more often. Princesses Desirée and Christina both live in Sweden. Christina, in particular, maintains close contact with the King's family. The two families have children of the same age.

Friends and relatives

Carl Gustaf and Silvia are both very sociable people. They have a wide circle of acquaintances, including in particular the King's old friends and their wives. In recent years they have widened their immediate circle to include, among others, businessman Arne Naess and his wife, the singer Diana Ross.

The Royal Family usually takes a trip each summer in *Ancylus*, the King's large motor yacht. On these occasions they live like any other family of holidaymakers. They sleep on board and are usually accompanied by friends and their children so that Victoria, Carl Philip and Madeleine have the company of children their own age. With the exception of security guards, there are no staff on board, and everybody has to take turns doing the shopping, cooking and washing the dishes and clothes.

The children's grandparents and other relatives visit the family at Solliden. This is the Royal couple's only completely private home, where they have nothing at all to do with official duties.

Although there are staff at Solliden, the Royal Family's guests must be prepared to lend a hand with the chores. The King's friends usually have to earn their keep by repairing a fence, painting, or helping to build a jetty, a bathing cabin or a fish smoking hut. Carl Gustaf has been keen on carpentry since early childhood, and at Solliden he gets his fill of it. There is always something to be done in or around the house and its grounds.

The Easter skiing holiday at the chalet in Storlien, in the mountains of north-west Sweden, is a well-established family tradition. All the Royal children learned to ski at an early age, and regularly join their parents on the slopes below

Pressens Bild

He usually takes the boat out early in the morning to set his nets. The catch generally consists of flounders, which are smoked in the hut on the jetty and eaten for lunch. Family dinners are often prepared by the King on the outdoor barbecue grill.

Victoria's birthday

The only official duty during the summer is Crown Princess Victoria's birthday. She marks the occasion by presenting a diploma and scholarship to the year's outstanding sportsman. The event is popular with local people and tourists, who turn out in good numbers to wish her 'Happy Birthday'.

As Victoria will one day be Queen, her parents are keen that she should familiarize herself with the responsibilities of public life and Royal duties from an early age.

Crown Princess Victoria celebrated her 13th birthday in 1990 and missed the annual birthday party on Öland for the first time. She was enjoying herself at a riding camp in the USA. Carl Philip, who was aged 11, was also

♔ *The Royal Family spend their summers at Solliden, the estate which Carl Gustaf inherited from his great-grandfather. Solliden is a haven from the responsibilities of royalty, where the King and Queen can relax in a completely informal atmosphere* **above**

♔ *The Detroit-born singer Diana Ross became friendly with the Royal couple following her marriage to the Swedish businessman Arne Naess. In 1986 she and Carl Gustaf jointly presented a cheque for 250,000 krone to the World Wide Fund for Nature* **right**

away from home at the time. He spent a fortnight at a sailing school instead. Madeleine is coming up to an age when she, too, will take holidays away from home. She plans to go to a riding camp in Sweden with Victoria.

The children's education

When Victoria was small her parents said they would like her to have as normal an upbringing as possible. They sent her to an ordinary local school, in a residential district close to Drottningholm. Carl Philip and Madeleine are now pupils at the same school.

The Royal couple appealed to teachers and parents not to make a fuss of the Royal children. To the surprise of many, this has worked extremely well. After a few days Victoria's classmates forgot she was a Princess, and even though they are impressed by her living in a Palace they do not consider her to be particularly spoilt.

The Royal couple attend parents' meetings like other parents and show a keen interest in their children's schooling. The children are, of course, allowed to invite their school-friends home. Carl Philip loves playing football with his classmates, while Victoria has several young friends who are every bit as mad about horses as she herself is.

The Crown Princess

Crown Princess Victoria is a very sweet girl who has her mother's brown eyes and her father's wavy fair hair. She is wise and sensible, as older sisters often are, and takes care of her brother and sister with a firm hand. Like Madeleine, her younger sister, she started riding when she was four and is now a skilful rider. She has won several jumping contests with Don Petit, a horse given to her as a birthday present by an Öland farmer. She also has a dog of her own called Sissi, a little brown and white

NATIONAL DAY

Sweden's National Day is celebrated on 6 June and although it is a working day there are usually processions and celebrations in most towns and villages. Queen Silvia has endeared herself to the Swedish people by wearing national costume on this day *right*. For women, this includes a flared skirt, apron, waistcoat and bonnet; men wear a folk costume of embroidered waistcoat, knee breeches and felt hat. Each province or town has its own particular variations, often indicated by intricate needlework designs. Specific floral patterns on a girl's waistcoat signify her place of birth and her marital status

King Charles spaniel who usually follows her all over the place.

The Royal couple were not particularly happy when the order of succession was changed, as they would have preferred to see Prince Carl Philip inherit the crown. This is not because they have any doubts as to how Victoria will cope with the task of being Queen. The problem is,they feel that it will be difficult for her to find a potential husband who is prepared to accept the subordinate role of Prince Consort. They would have wished her to be in a more favourable position when the time came for her to get married.

To be on the safe side, Prince Carl Philip is being raised in the same way as Victoria. He must get used to carrying out minor official duties and will gradually shoulder more and more responsibilities. The Prince is a nice little chap, tender, lively and charming. He loves going to ice hockey and football matches with his father and is more interested in animals and the countryside than in cars and boats.

A young scamp

Madeleine is the family clown and scamp. The two older children are very obedient and polite, but Madeleine does exactly as she pleases. Of course, she is spoilt by her parents and brother and sister, and she knows that they have difficulty in keeping a straight face when she plays the fool. She is very lively and quite stubborn, and does not mind getting dirty, tearing her stockings or losing the ribbon from her hair. She is for ever climbing about or running and skipping, and never sits still for long. She can twist her father round her little finger, but

she knows from experience that her mother can occasionally be really angry and will give her a sharp talking to.

Crown Princess Victoria started at a Stockholm private school in autumn 1990, when she became too old for her former school. The Royal couple were against putting her into a boarding school and would have preferred not to send her to a private school. But it proved quite difficult to find a suitable state school in central Stockholm that is easy to guard. For that reason, the choice fell on Carlsson's School, which Princess Christina's three sons already attended.

Victoria will change school again in 1992, when she is old enough for secondary school. When that time comes, Victoria will be given a say in the matter. She and her brother and sister will presumably study abroad to improve their knowledge of languages. A newly-employed English nanny, Beverly Smith, is already teaching the children English.

A new member of the family

A further member was added to the Royal Family in 1987. Silvia's brother Walther is divorced and his son Patrick was in need of security and support. Naturally Silvia answered the call and the lad was invited to stay at Drottningholm and start at a local school. He got on famously and matriculated at Bromma in spring 1990. Patrick visited his parents in Paris for the summer, and will complete his studies in Sweden.

The children thought it was wonderful to have a 'big brother', and no doubt the Royal couple also found it reassuring to have him in the house when they were away travelling. He

♛ *Queen Silvia's German parentage has helped to seal friendly relations between the two countries. She acted as hostess at the State banquet for Richard von Weizsacker, President of the Federal Republic of Germany, and his wife, during their visit in 1988* above

ROYAL VISIT TO THE USA

When King Carl Gustaf and Queen Silvia visited the United States in the spring of 1988, it was more than just an ordinary State visit. The 17-day Royal tour commemorated 'New Sweden 88', the anniversary of the founding of the 17th-century Swedish colony in America. President Reagan had proclaimed 1988 New Sweden Year to draw attention to the part played by Sweden in the early history of the USA.

The tour was not only a goodwill visit but also a public relations exercise, promoting Swedish trade, industry and culture. The Royal couple visited 17 places between Washington and Los Angeles, met thousands of people and were seen on television by millions of Americans. They were entertained by President and Mrs Reagan in the White House *right*, attended a Texas rodeo and went to a Hollywood film party. The visit was a huge success; Sweden had presented itself as a go-

ahead, high-technology country producing first-class products, while the King and Queen greatly impressed the American people with their natural charm and spontaneity

🜲 *Silvia's nephew, Patrick, the son of her divorced brother, has lived with the Royal Family, taking on the role of elder brother to his young cousins, since 1987. In 1990 the family all congratulated him on his matriculation below. Also part of the wider family circle are several dogs; Crown Princess Victoria has a spaniel of her own, but is seen playing above right with the family's labrador*

kept an eye on his cousins and was on hand when they began missing their parents.

So that everything runs smoothly, even when the Royal couple are away, a governess will soon be engaged to help the children with their lessons.

A warm relationship

Silvia and Carl Gustaf will have been married for 15 years in 1991. The early infatuation has turned into a warm and loyal relationship. It is difficult to know whether they are really happy with each other, as they seldom show any signs of affection in public. But they do exchange glances and smiles, whisper confidences and appear to still enjoy each other's company.

Once or twice a year they treat themselves to a romantic holiday, even if only for a few days. They generally travel abroad incognito. Sometimes they visit London to shop and eat out, and sometimes they choose the Riviera, where Prince Bertil has a magnificent villa. They have also had good times together in New York and have enjoyed bathing holidays and family visits in Brazil.

Now that the couple have three children it is becoming increasingly difficult for them to get away. They feel they are needed at home because new things are happening to the children every day, which they are eager to tell their parents about.

Two determined characters

No doubt Carl Gustaf and Silvia have had slumps in their marriage, just like everyone else. The King is rather stubborn and is used to having his own way. He can get very irritated when things go against him and tends to become sulky and arrogant.

Silvia is also a very determined person, who knows exactly what she wants. She is admittedly more diplomatic than her husband, but if an issue is important to her she refuses to give in.

The King enjoys living life to the full. He is fond of good food and wine, appreciates beautiful girls and still likes going to discos. He likes having a good time with his friends, and his parties usually last till dawn.

Silvia does not always approve of the King's friends. Some of the more notorious partygoers in the King's circle disappeared rather quickly when he got married. Nevertheless, many people point out that Silvia is really tremendously loyal and helpful. When people are in trouble it is invariably she who comes forward to console and help them.

THE POPE'S VISIT TO SWEDEN

Pope John Paul II visited Stockholm in June 1989. It was an historic occasion for, although Sweden is a Christian but not noticeably religious country, 15,000 people attended the mass given by the Pope in Stockholm's Globe. The Pope also officiated at a service in Uppsala Cathedral and met the Royal Family *below* who were impressed and honoured by the warmth and obvious piety of His Holiness

Silvia is more serious than her husband by nature, and she takes her responsibilities as Queen, wife and mother very seriously. People who work with her will testify that she is practically a perfectionist and has an excellent memory for people and information.

Changed

Perhaps the radiantly happy and spontaneous girl who was introduced as Carl Gustaf's fiancée no longer exists. Silvia Sommerlath has grown into her role of Queen. She observes protocol, does her job to perfection, and everyone who meets her is charmed by her wonder-

Syndication International

ful smile and her genuine interest in people. But some of the happiness appears to have vanished under the pressure of her demanding new roles.

The strains Silvia experiences are those of any talented career woman who is also a wife and mother, but for her there is the added pressure of always being in the public eye. The carefree happiness she exhibited in her youth has, not unnaturally, been tempered by the responsibilities of later life.

Silvia herself admits that she has changed: 'It is difficult to say in what way I have changed. I have developed and I think perhaps I am a little deeper. My life is rich and enriching, and it has given me some great experiences. The children have opened up a new world and given my life a new meaning. It is wonderful to feel alive and know that I am needed.'

She has changed in some ways but the essential Silvia is still the same as she ever was: 'Inside I am the Silvia I have always been and hope to remain. I realise that a person in my

👑 *In 1989 the Royal Family broke with tradition by posing for their portraits in the grounds of Drottningholm Palace, with Lake Malaren sparkling in the background* top, *rather than at Solliden. As their children grow, and begin to find new interests outside the home, Sweden's King and Queen spend an increasing amount of time simply enjoying one another's company* above

position can easily lose their foothold. I fight hard to preserve my identity and I admit quite frankly that it is difficult.'

Gains and losses

One suspects there have been times when Silvia has longed for her former life as an unknown girl in Heidelberg. Perhaps she occasionally wishes that she had married an ordinary man and been able to raise her children to a free life, one which would have allowed them to decide their own future.

It would be surprising if that were not the case. However, her present life, exacting though it is, has many compensations. She is

'Inside I am the Silvia I have always been and hope to remain'

SILVIA

well off and can enjoy the pleasures of luxury homes, fashionable clothes, exotic holidays and a freedom from financial worries. She also clearly enjoys the work she does and the opportunity to meet a wide cross-section of people from around the world. Her position gives her the chance to talk with leading politicians, athletes, scientists, musicians and many others at the top of their professions.

She has also gained admittance to an exclusive club – the world of royalty – and can mingle with crowned heads on equal terms. Many girls may dream of becoming a Princess or a Queen but few are fortunate enough to realize that dream – and fewer still make such an outstanding success of the reality.